Flute Time Christmas

a stockingful of 32 easy pieces for flute

Kathy and David Blackwell

with Caroline Hobbs-Smith

illustrations by Alan Rowe

Welcome to **Flute Time Christmas**. You'll find:

- 32 well-known Christmas carols and pieces with words to sing along
- solos and duets
- easy chord symbols for guitar or keyboard accompaniment; these chords are not compatible with the CD performances
- a CD with performances to listen or play along to; the varied accompaniments use piano, guitar, drums, and bass
- piano accompaniments available in a separate volume

Using the CD:

- all carols and pieces are played through twice, except those pieces which include a **D.C.** or **D.S. al Fine**, 'Skaters' Waltz', and 'Hogmanay Reel', which are performed once only
- each carol and piece has a short introduction and a link between the verses
- where there are duet parts, these are mostly added in the second verse
- Tuning track: track 33.

Performers: flute Caroline Hobbs-Smith; guitar Jez Cook; double bass/bass guitar Mike Chilcott; percussion/drum kit Ben Twyford; piano David Blackwell.

MUSIC DEPARTMENT

OXFORD
UNIVERSITY PRESS

T0056057

UNIVERSITY PRESS

Great Clarendon Street, Oxford OX2 6DP, England

Oxford University Press is a department of the University of Oxford.
It furthers the University's aim of excellence in research, scholarship,
and education by publishing worldwide

7 9 10 8

ISBN 978–0–19–337927–5

Music and text origination by
Katie Johnston
Printed in Great Britain on acid-free paper by
Halstan & Co. Ltd, Amersham, Bucks.

Contents

* These carols can be played an octave higher for the second verse.

1. Hark! the herald-angels sing

Felix Mendelssohn (1809–47)

Hark! the he - rald - an-gels sing_ Glo-ry to the new-born King; Peace on earth and mer-cy mild,_ God and sin - ners re - con-ciled: Joy-ful all ye na-tions rise,_ Join the tri-umph of the skies, With the'an-gel - ic host pro-claim, Christ is_ born in Beth-le-hem. Hark! the he-rald - an-gels sing Glo-ry_ to the new-born King.

2. Mary had a baby

American trad.

Ma-ry had a ba - by, Yes, Lord! Ma-ry had a ba - by, Yes, my Lord! Ma-ry had a ba - by, Yes, Lord! Peo-ple keep a-com-in', and the train done gone!

The hol - ly and the i - vy When they are both full

grown; Of___ all the trees that are in the wood The___ hol - ly bears the

crown. The ris - ing of the sun___ And the run-ning of the

deer, The___ play-ing of the mer-ry or - gan, Sweet sing-ing in the choir.

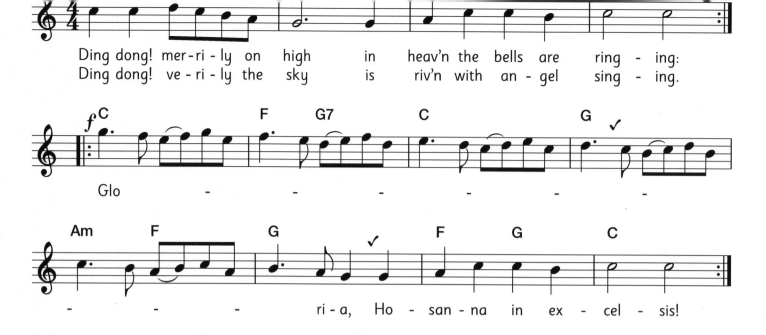

Ding dong! mer-ri-ly on high in heav'n the bells are ring - ing:
Ding dong! ve-ri-ly the sky is riv'n with an - gel sing - ing.

Glo - - - - - - - -

- - - ri - a, Ho - san - na in ex - cel - sis!

5. Andrew mine, Jasper mine

Moravian carol

Simply

An - drew mine, Jas - per mine, Ti - mo - thy and A - bel,

Hur - ry to Beth - le - hem, to the com - mon sta - ble.

There you'll find a ba - by small, sleep - ing in a swad-dling shawl;

On your way, on your way, to our Sa - viour born to - day.

Andrew mine, Jasper mine: words by C. K. Offer from *Three Moravian Carols* © Oxford University Press 1962. Reproduced by permission of Oxford University Press.

6. Silent night

Franz Gruber (1787–1863)

Si - lent night, ho - ly night, All is calm,
all is bright; Round yon vir - gin mo - ther and child.
Ho - ly in - fant so ten - der and mild, Sleep in
hea - ven-ly peace,___ Sleep___ in hea - ven-ly peace.

7. I saw three ships

English trad.

Like a dance

I saw three ships come sail-ing in On Christ-mas Day, on Christ-mas Day, I

saw three ships come sail-ing in On Christ-mas Day in the morn - ing.

8. O little town of Bethlehem

English trad.

Gently

O lit - tle town of Beth - le - hem, How still we__ see thee lie!
A - bove thy deep and dream-less sleep The si - lent stars go by.

Yet__ in thy dark streets shin - eth The ev - er - last-ing light; The

hopes and fears of all__ the__ years Are met in__ thee to - night.

9. Christmas Calypso

Kathy & David Blackwell

Happily

So dance the | Christ-mas Ca-lyp-so | in the sun,—

Je-sus is born for | ev-'ry-one;— | Sing out with joy and

stamp your feet,— | move to the ca- | lyp-so beat!— **Fine**

Way back in | Beth-le-hem,_ | in a sim-ple | sta-ble,

Je-sus, that | ba-by boy,_ | came to save us | all! So dance the

D.% al Fine

10. Once in royal David's city

H. J. Gauntlett (1805–76)

Gently

Once in roy - al Da - vid's ci - ty Stood a low - ly cat - tle_ shed,
Where a mo - ther laid_ her_ ba - by In a man - ger for_ his_ bed:

Ma - ry was that mo - ther mild, Je - sus Christ her lit - tle_ child.

11. Go tell it on the mountain

American trad.

With energy

Go tell it on the moun - tain, o - ver the hills and ev - 'ry - where;

Go tell it on the moun - tain that Je - sus Christ is born!

Shep-herds kept their watch - ing o'er wand-'ring flocks by night; Be -

-hold from out of hea - ven there shone a ho - ly light:_____

We wish you a mer-ry Christ-mas, We wish you a mer-ry Christ-mas, We
wish you a mer-ry Christ-mas And a hap-py New Year. Good
ti-dings we bring To you and your kin; We
wish you a mer-ry Christ-mas And a hap-py New Year.

14. Shepherds watched

Czech carol

Shep-herds watched their lambs and sheep, Through the night so dark and deep.

Lo, the an-gel in the skies, Bid-ding them to stand and rise.

Hi-dom, hi-dom, hi-do-dom, Hi-dom, hi-dom, hi-do-dom.

Hi-dom, hi-dom, hi-do-dom, Hi-dom, hi-dom, hi-do-dom.

15. We three kings

J. H. Hopkins (1820–91)

We three kings of O - ri - ent are; Bear - ing gifts we tra - verse a - far Field and foun - tain, moor and moun - tain, Fol - low - ing yon - der star: O____ star of won - der, star of night, Star with roy - al beau - ty bright, West - ward lead - ing, still pro - ceed - ing, Guide us to thy per - fect light.

16. O come, all ye faithful

J. F. Wade (c.1711–86)

17. Bethl'em lay a-sleeping

Polish carol

Simply

mp

Beth - l'em lay a - sleep - ing, long, so long a - go,

Twink - ling stars were peep - ing, long, so long a - go,

When to earth a ba - by came, lit - tle Je - sus was his name, long, long a - go.

18. Deck the hall

Welsh trad.

Lively

Deck the hall with boughs of hol - ly, Fa la la la la, fa la la la;

'Tis the sea - son to be jol - ly, Fa la la la la, fa la la la.

Fill the mead cup, drain the bar - rel, Fa la la la la la la la la;

Troll the an - cient Christ-mas ca - rol, Fa la la la la, fa la la la.

19. Good King Wenceslas

Piae Cantiones (1582)

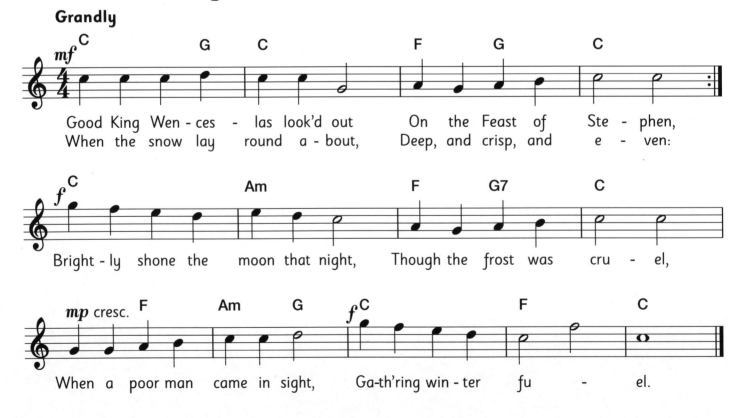

Grandly

Good King Wen - ces - las look'd out On the Feast of Ste - phen,
When the snow lay round a - bout, Deep, and crisp, and e - ven:

Bright - ly shone the moon that night, Though the frost was cru - el,

When a poor man came in sight, Ga-th'ring win - ter fu - el.

20. Away in a manger

William J. Kirkpatrick (1838–1921)

Tenderly

A - way in a__ man-ger, no__ crib for a bed, The__ lit - tle Lord
Je - sus laid__ down his sweet head; The stars in the__ bright sky looked
down where he lay, The__ lit - tle Lord Je - sus a - sleep on the hay.

21. The first Nowell

English trad.

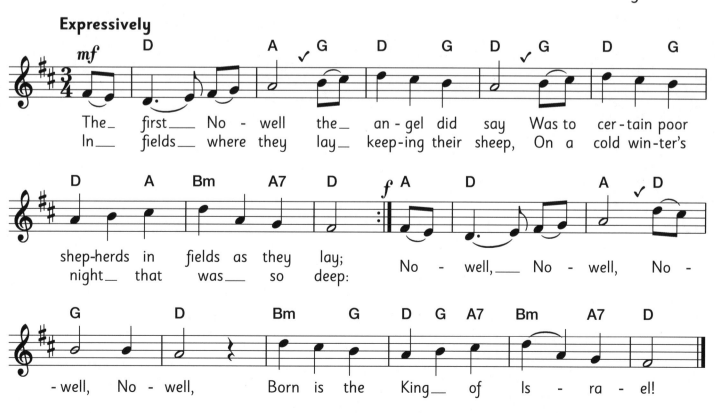

Expressively

The__ first__ No - well the__ an - gel did say Was to cer - tain poor
In__ fields__ where they lay__ keep-ing their sheep, On a cold win-ter's

shep-herds in fields as they lay; No - well,__ No - well, No -
night__ that was__ so deep:

- well, No - well, Born is the King__ of Is - ra - el!

22. Zither Carol

Czech carol

Brightly

Girls and boys, leave your toys, make no noise, Kneel at his crib and wor-ship him.

At thy shrine, child di-vine, we are thine, Our Sa-viour's here.

'Hal - le - lu - jah' the church bells ring, 'Hal - le - lu - jah' the an - gels sing,

'Hal - le - lu - jah' from ev - 'ry - thing. All must draw near.

23. God rest you merry, gentlemen

English trad.

On the move

God rest you mer - ry, gen - tle - men, Let no - thing you dis - may, For

Je - sus Christ our Sa - viour Was born up - on this day, To save us all from

Sa - tan's power When we were gone a - stray: O___ ti - dings of com - fort and

joy, com - fort and joy, O___ ti - dings of com - fort and joy.

24. While shepherds watched their flocks

Este's Psalter (1592)

Lively

While shep-herds watched their flocks by night, All seat-ed on the ground, The

an - gel of the Lord came down, And glo - ry shone a - round.

25. Children, go!

Spiritual

Lively

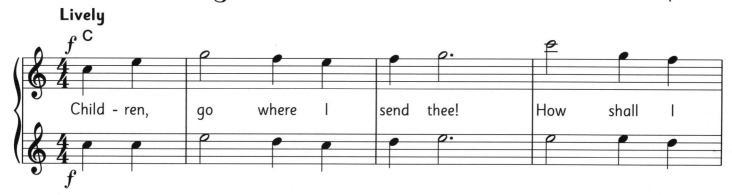

Child - ren, go where I send thee! How shall I

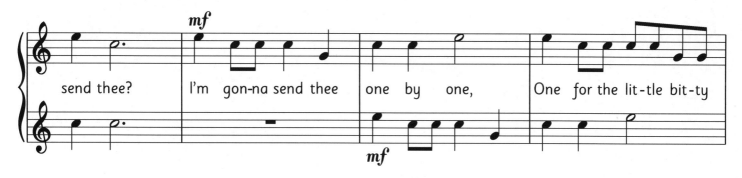

send thee? I'm gon-na send thee one by one, One for the lit-tle bit-ty

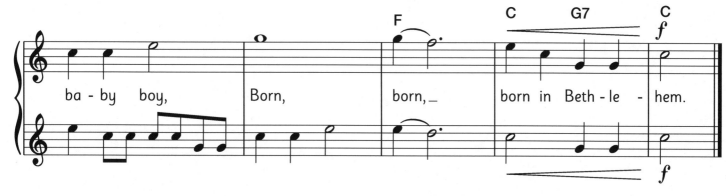

ba - by boy, Born, born,— born in Beth - le - hem.

26. Dance of the Reed Pipes

(from the *Nutcracker* ballet)

Pyotr Ilyich Tchaikovsky (1840–93)

Andante

mf sempre stacc.

cresc.

mf

27. Skaters' Waltz

Emil Waldteufel (1837–1915)

28. Jingle, bells

J. Pierpont (1822–93)

Happily

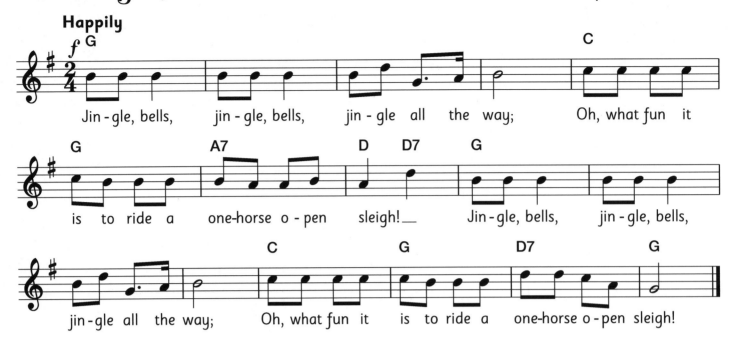

Jin-gle, bells, jin-gle, bells, jin-gle all the way; Oh, what fun it

is to ride a one-horse o-pen sleigh!__ Jin-gle, bells, jin-gle, bells,

jin-gle all the way; Oh, what fun it is to ride a one-horse o-pen sleigh!

29. Infant holy, infant lowly

Polish carol

Like a lullaby

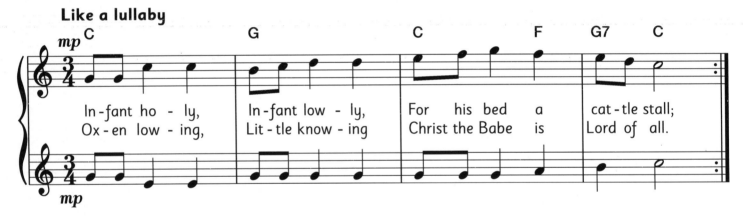

In-fant ho-ly, In-fant low-ly, For his bed a cat-tle stall;
Ox-en low-ing, Lit-tle know-ing Christ the Babe is Lord of all.

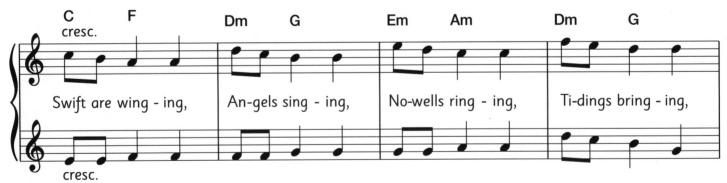

Swift are wing-ing, An-gels sing-ing, No-wells ring-ing, Ti-dings bring-ing,

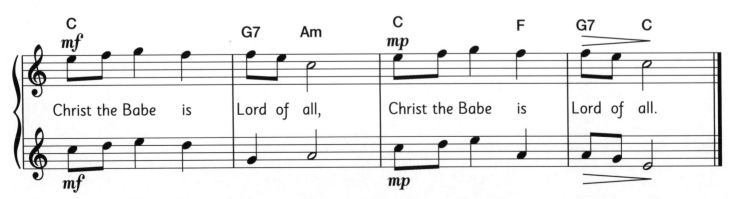

Christ the Babe is Lord of all, Christ the Babe is Lord of all.

30. Child in a manger

Celtic trad.

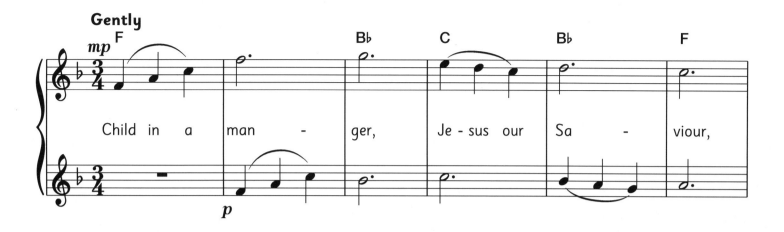

Child in a man - ger, Je - sus our Sa - viour,

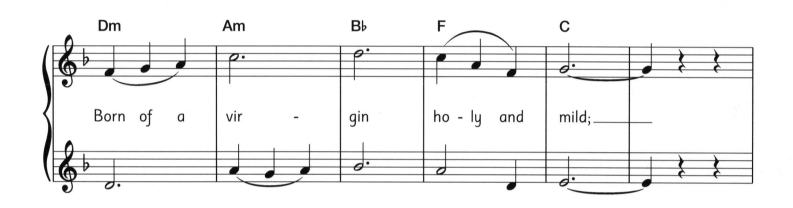

Born of a vir - gin ho - ly and mild;

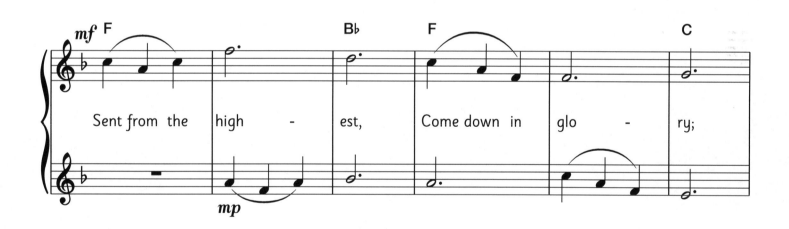

Sent from the high - est, Come down in glo - ry;

Tell the glad sto - ry, Wel-come the child.

31. Hogmanay Reel

Kathy & David Blackwell

With energy

32. Auld Lang Syne

Scottish trad.

With a wee dram!

Should auld ac-quain-tance be for-got, and_ nev - er brought to mind? Should

auld ac-quain-tance be for-got, for the sake of auld lang syne? For

auld___ lang___ syne, my dear, for auld___ lang___ syne; We'll

tak' a cup o' kind - ness yet, for the sake of auld lang syne.